Adult Coloring book Mixed

Vol 8

By: L. M. Boelz

I want to take a moment to thank you for purchasing this coloring book.

A lot of time went into the making of it. I wanted to be able to give you hours of fun

and relaxation. So Enjoy. Be sure to check out my other coloring books if you

like this one.   There are 28 different pictures to color in this book.

Other titles

Southwest, Floral, Chickens, Zen Eggs

Dragons Fantasy, Day of the Dead & Mardi Gras

Farm Animals, Hot Arizona Desert

This book contains a few more hand drawn pictures then the themed
books. You may see a few flaws I tried to get to them all, but it is the
nature of having hand drawn pictures to color.
They are not computer mass generated.

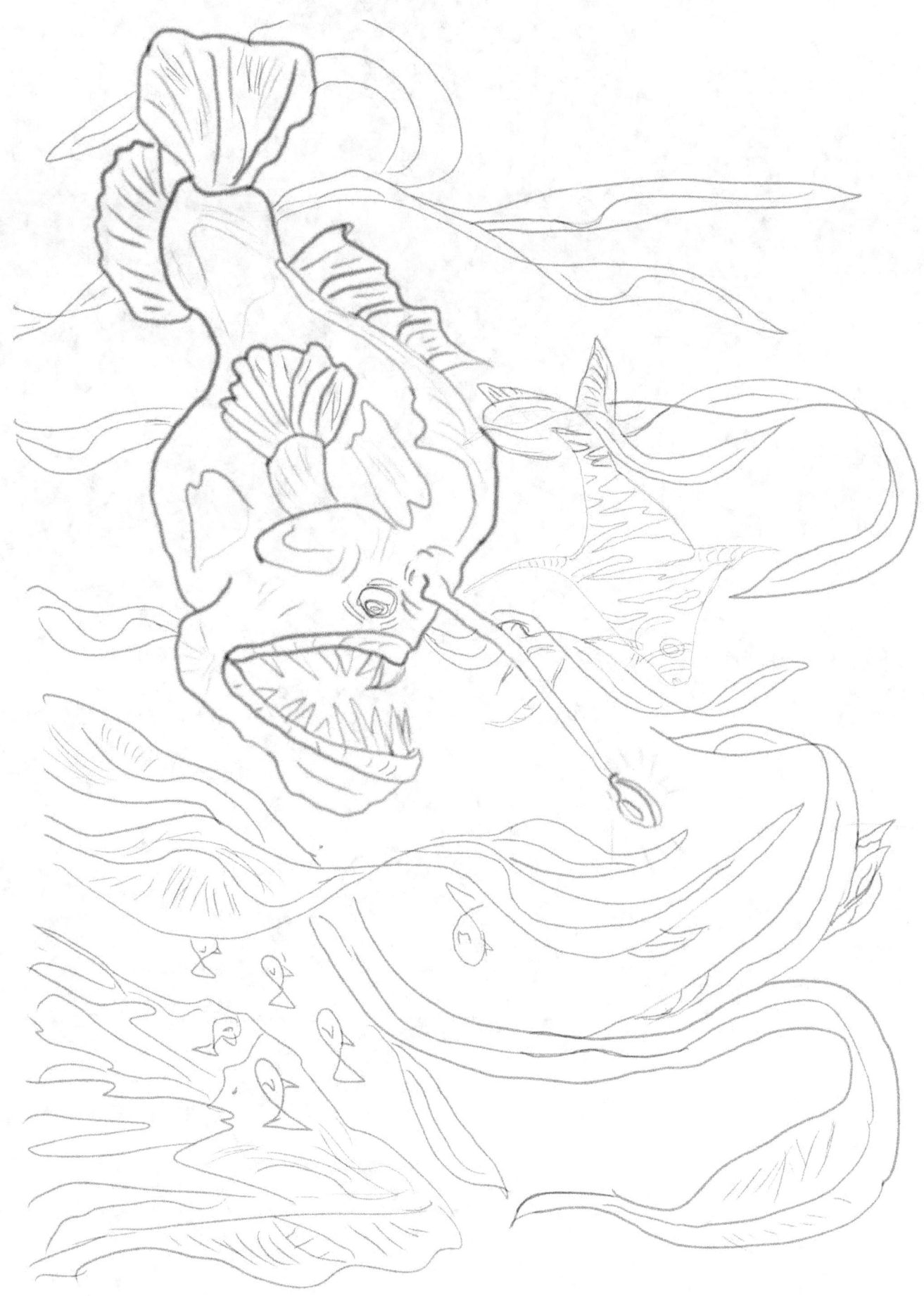

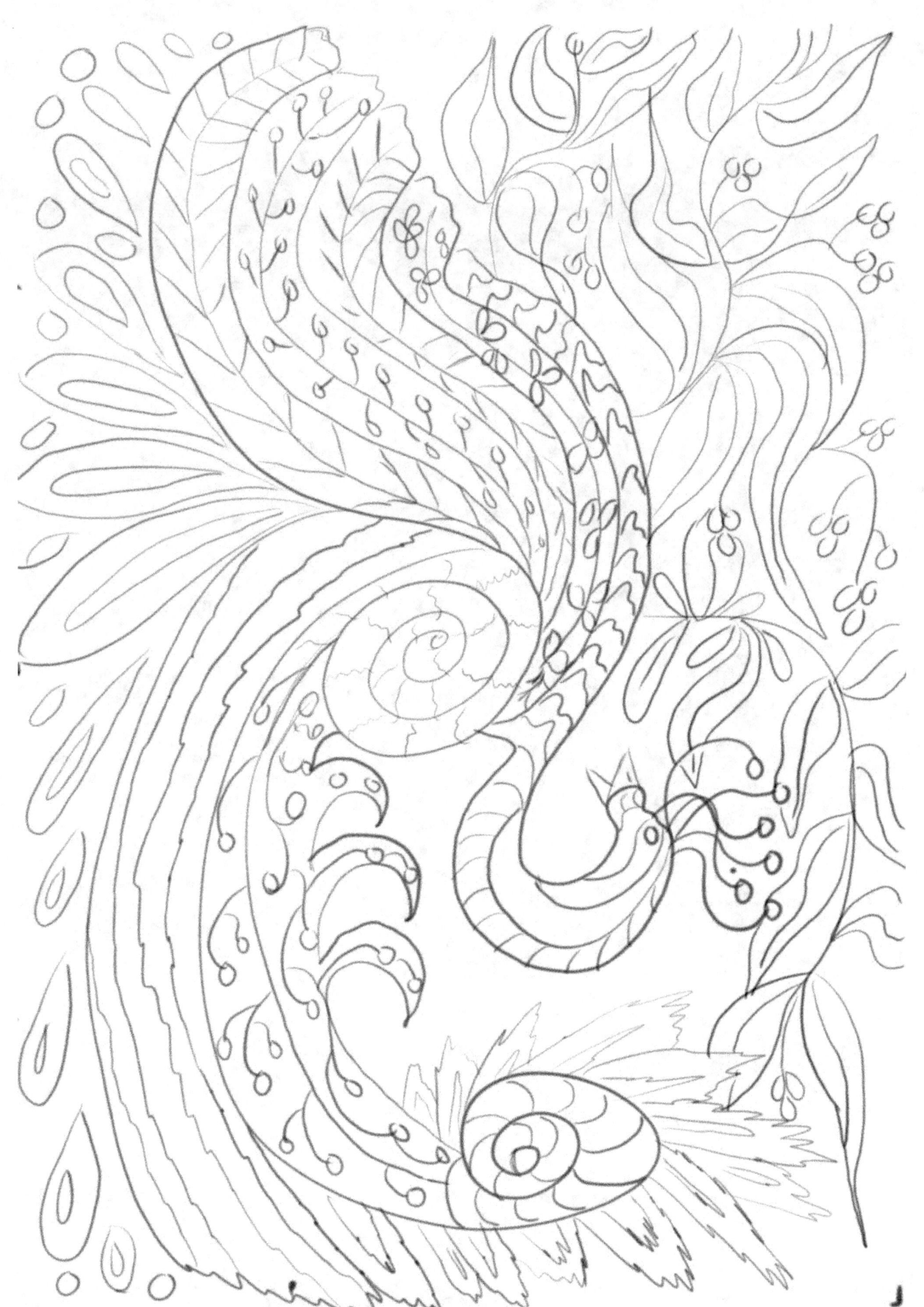

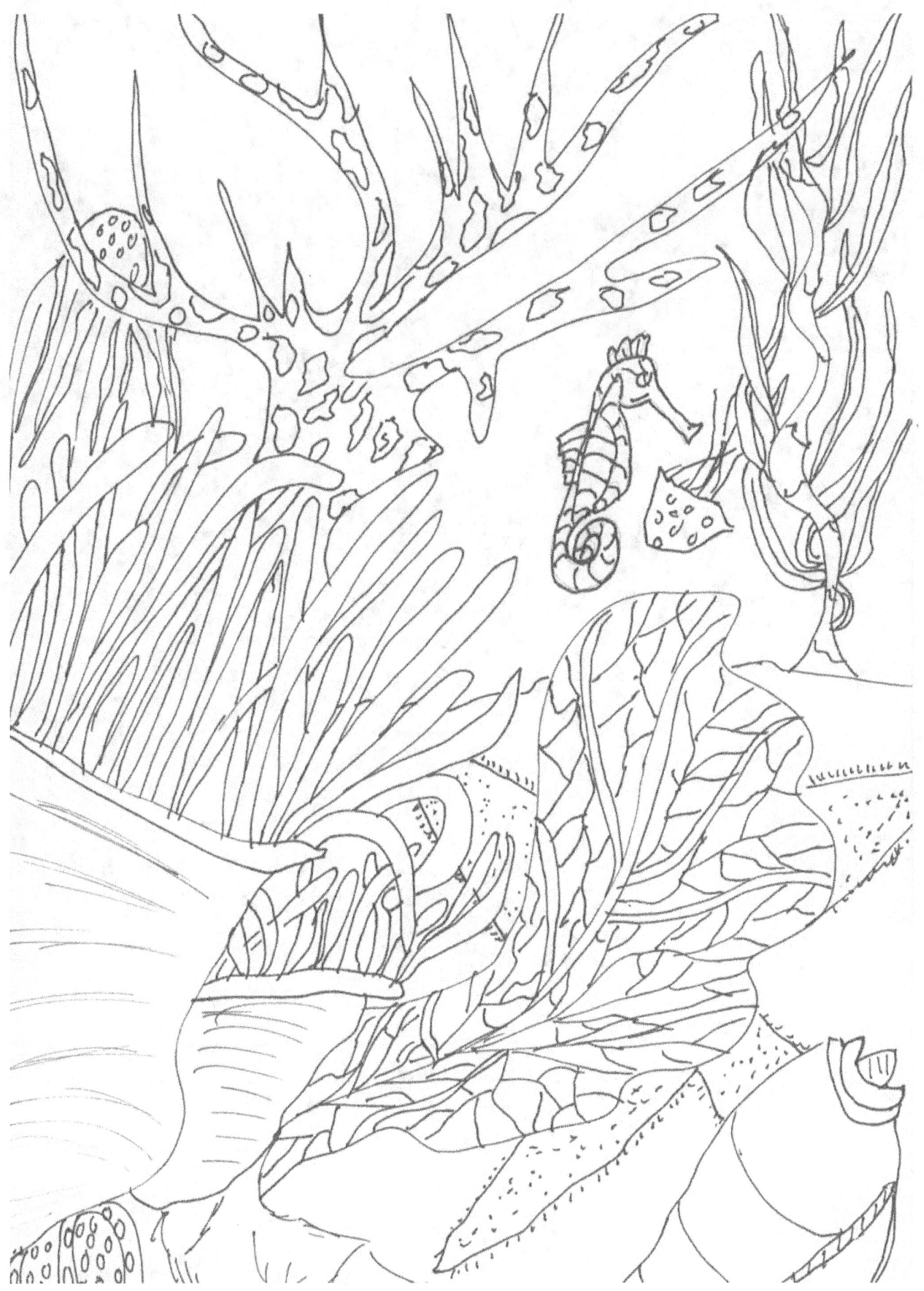

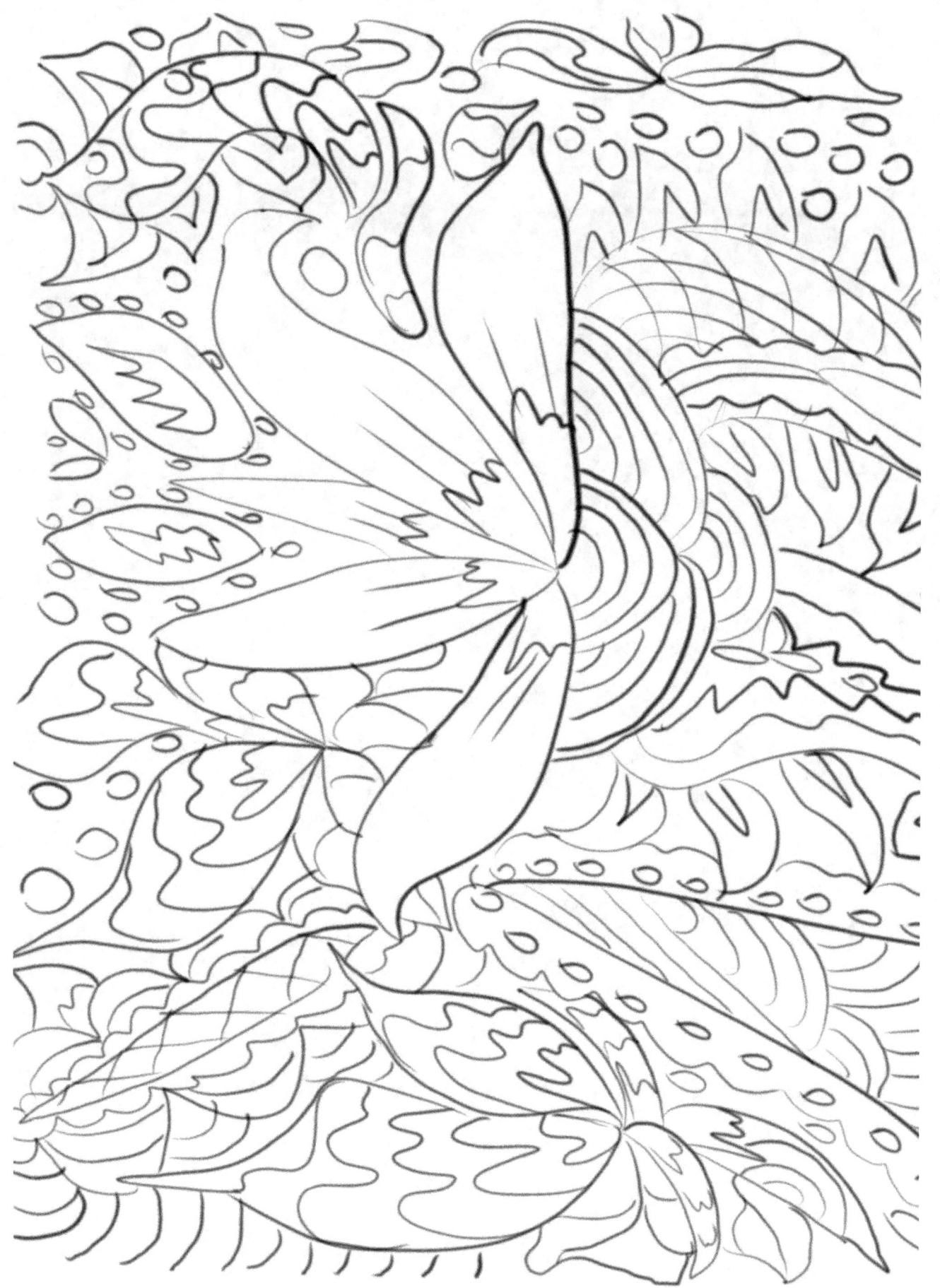

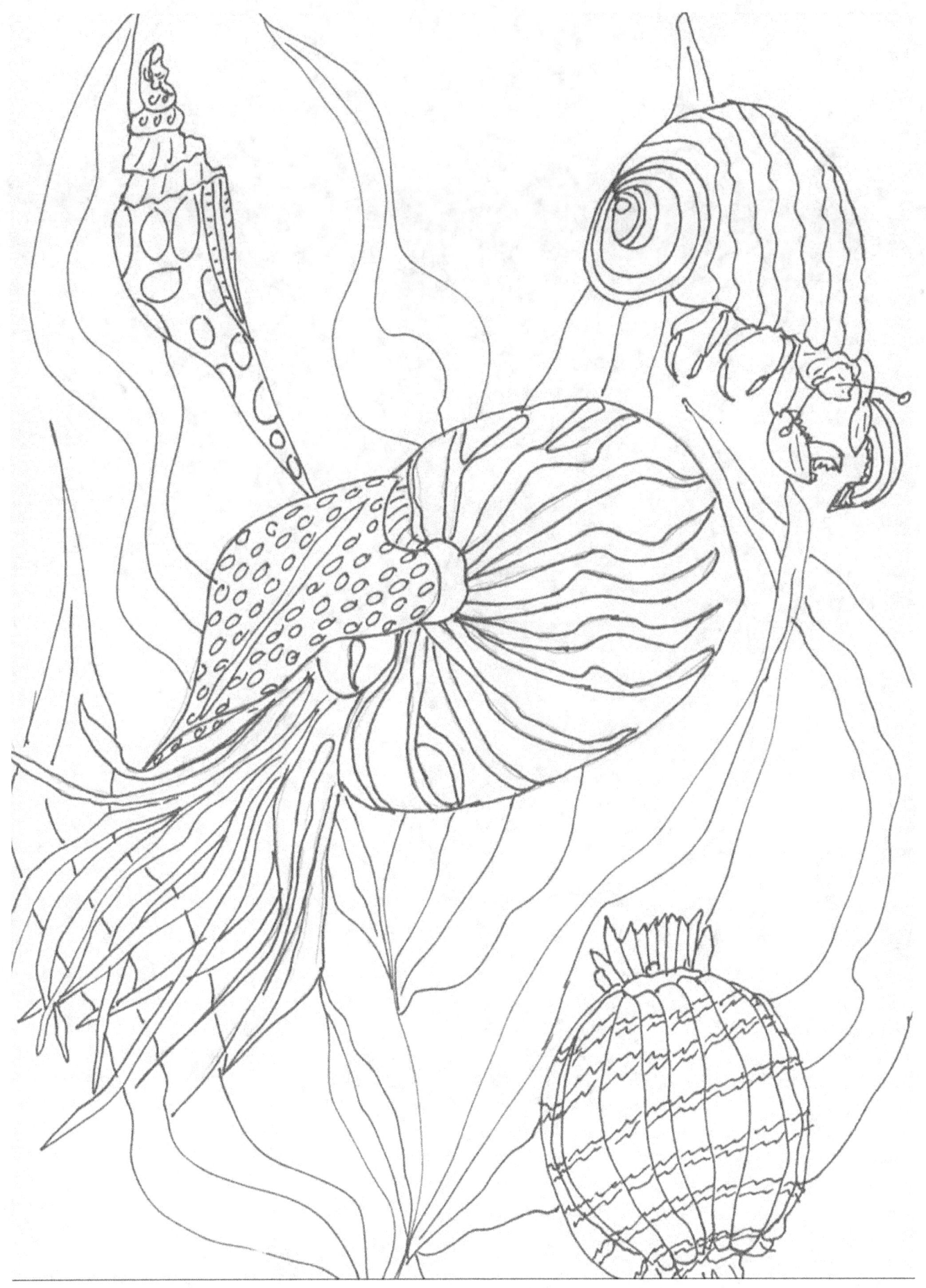

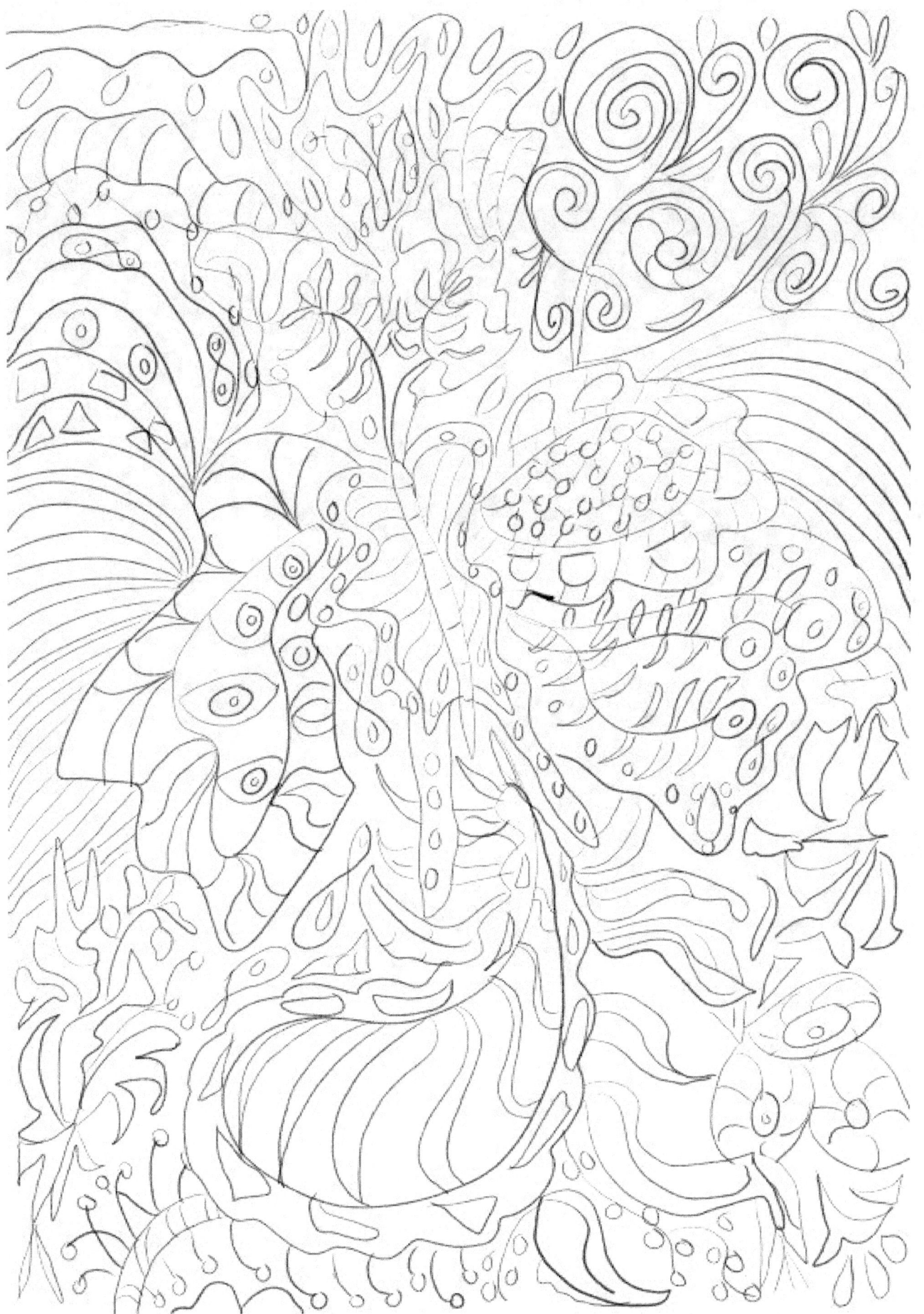

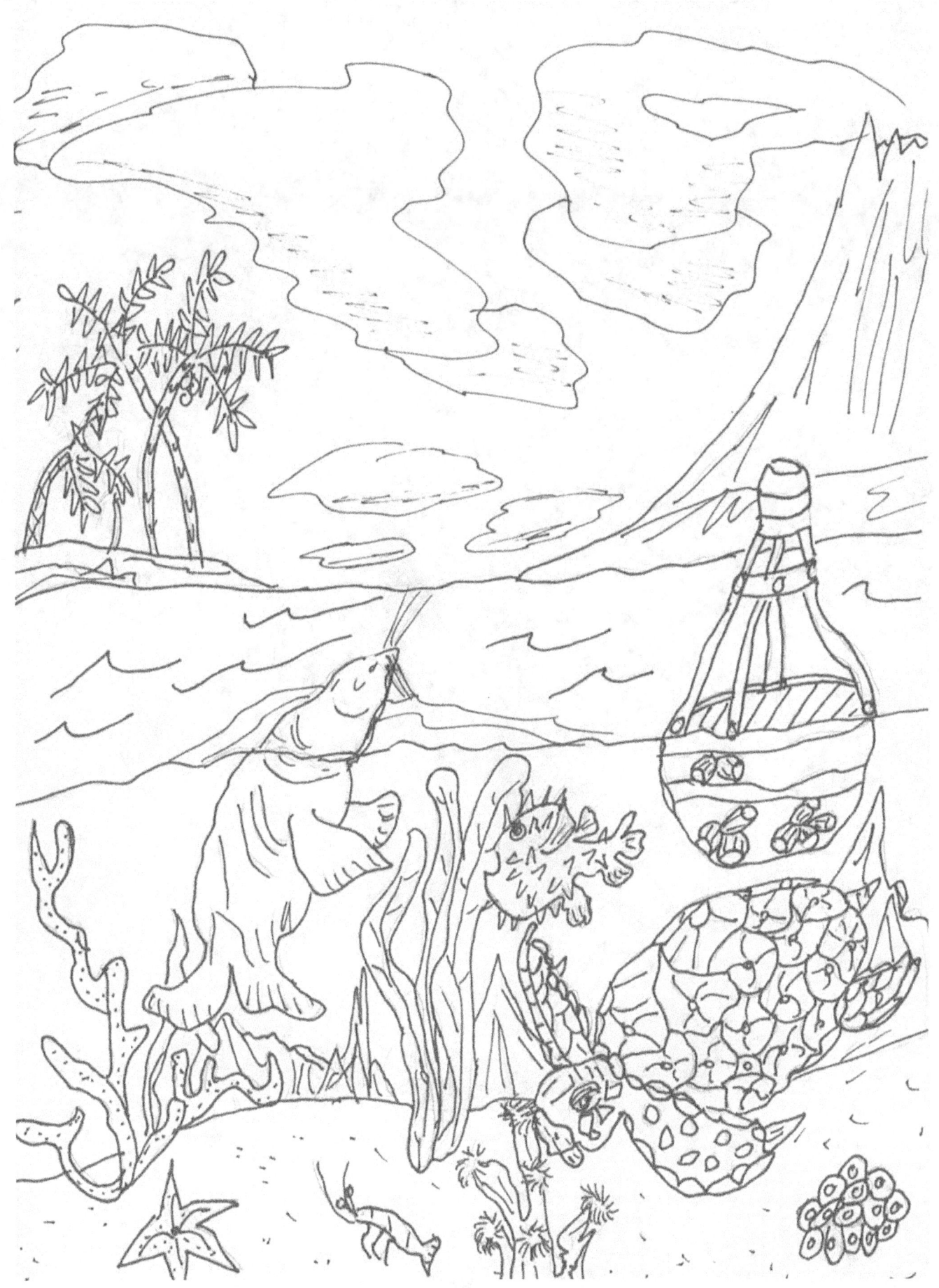

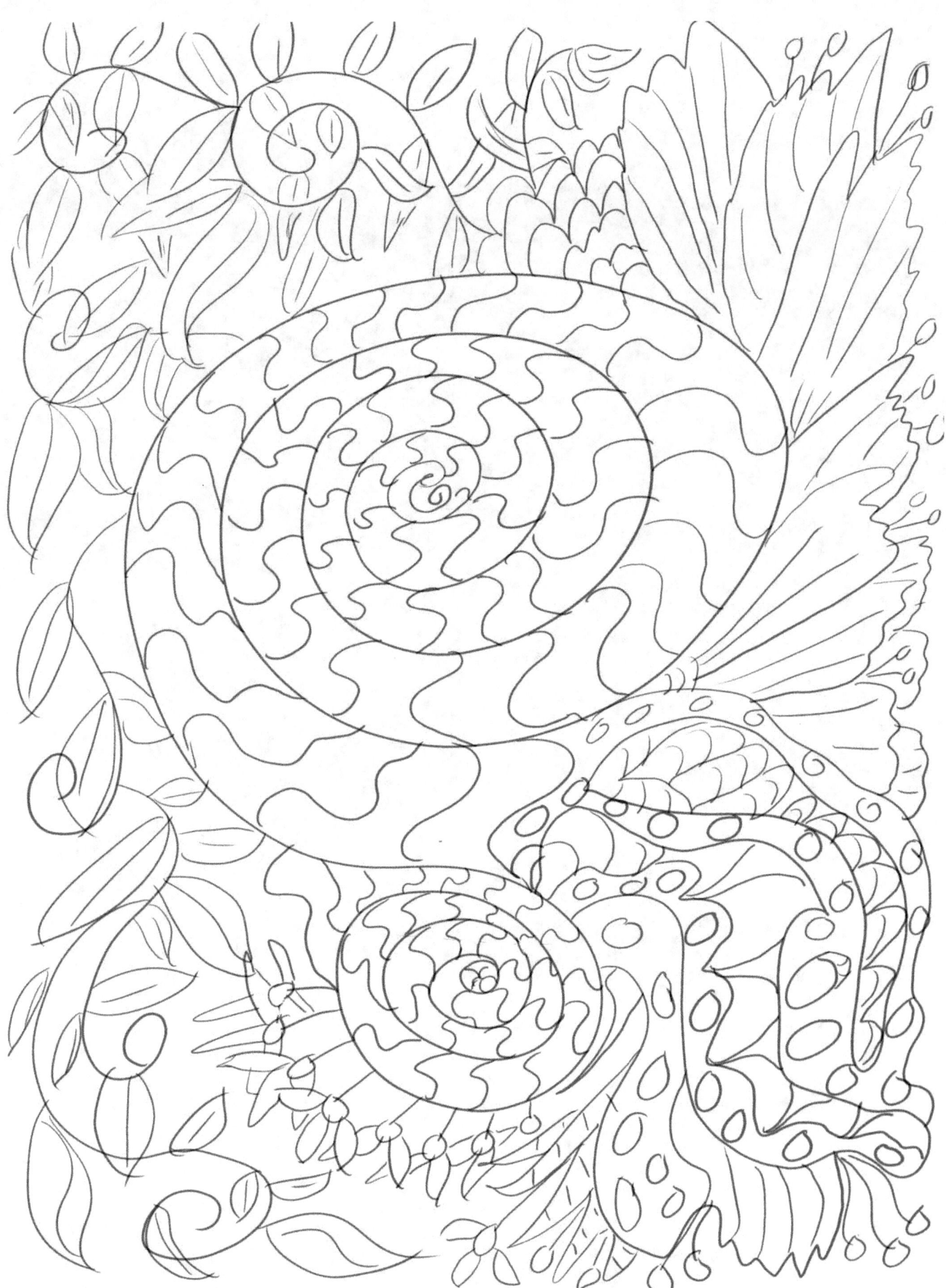

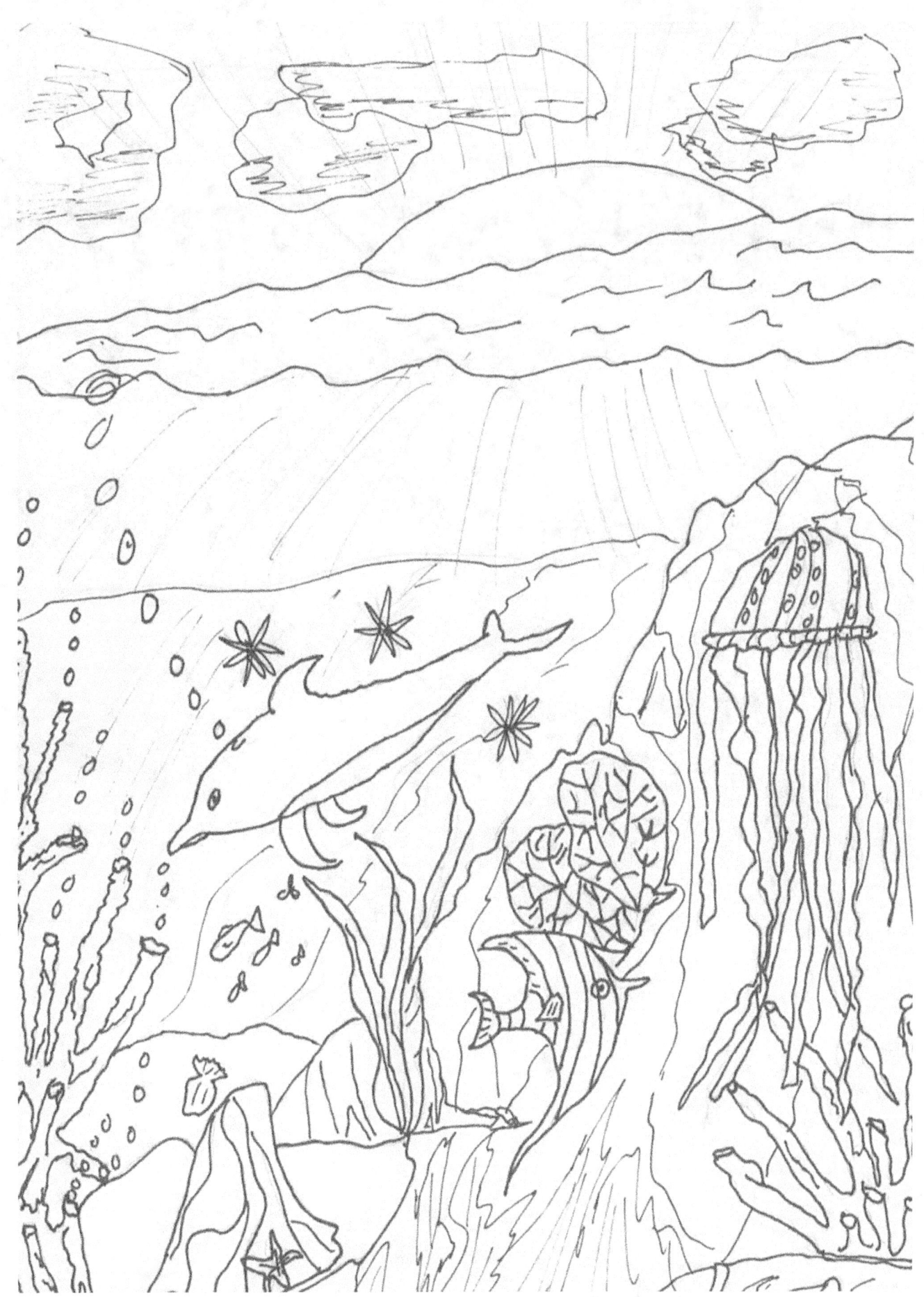

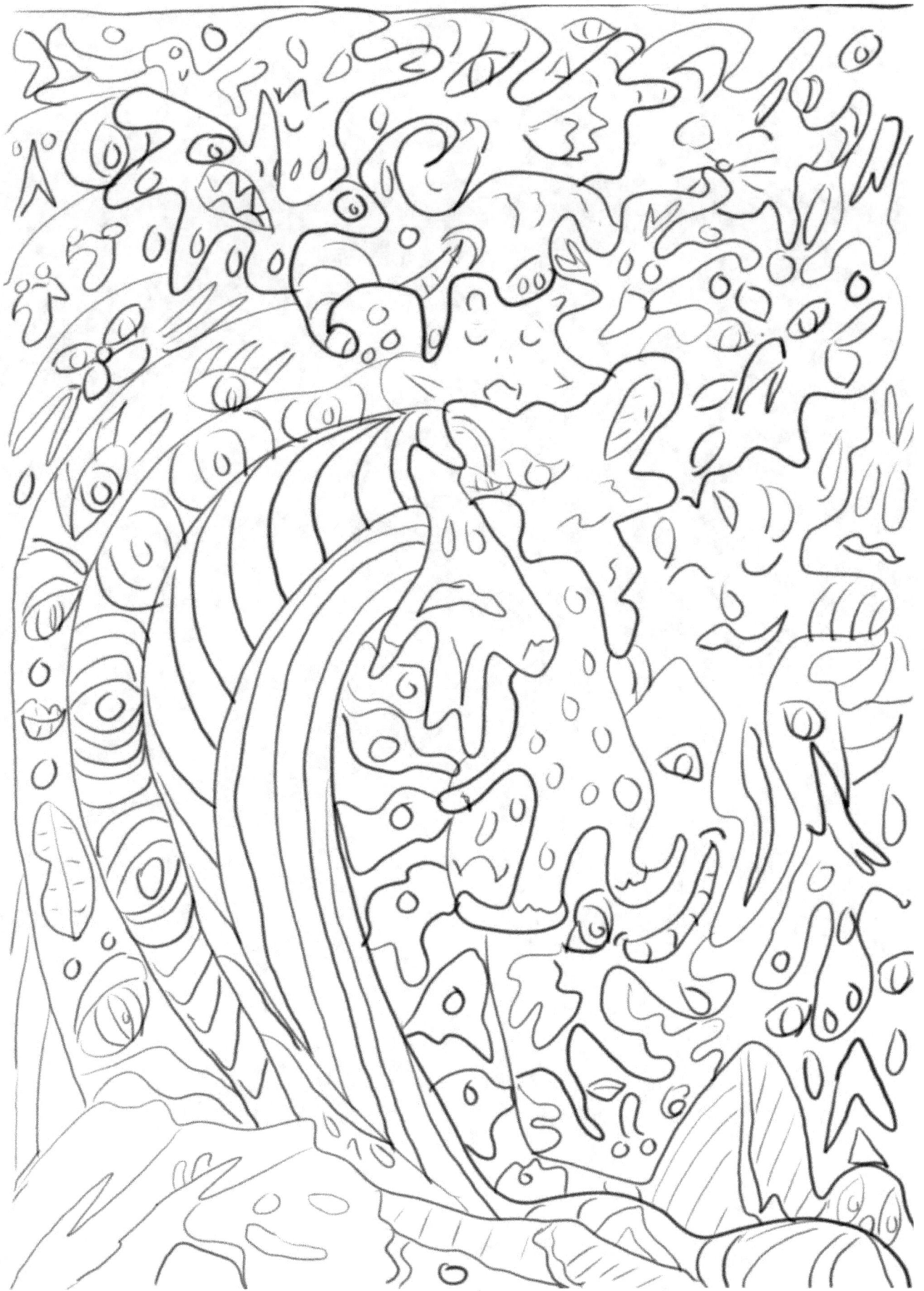

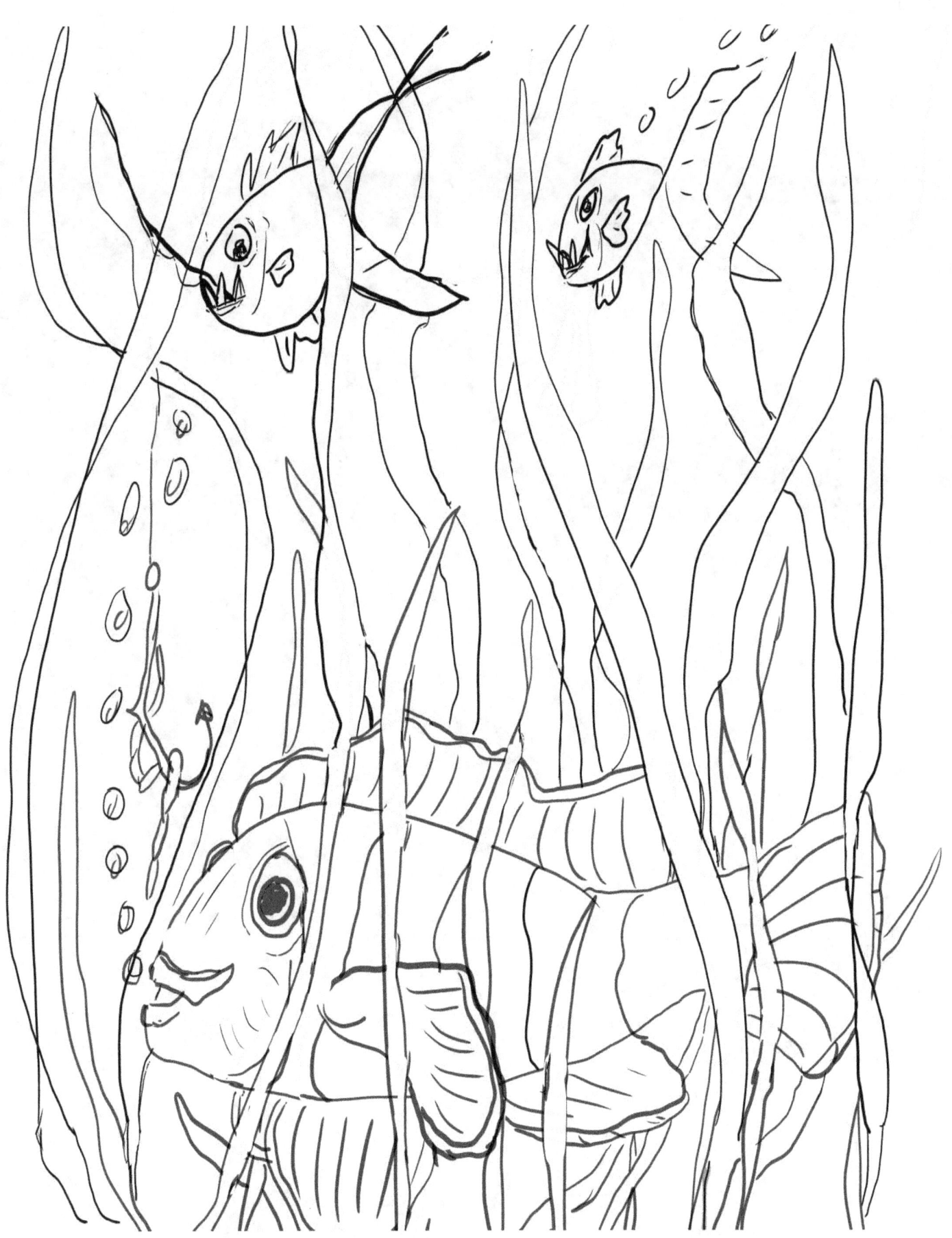

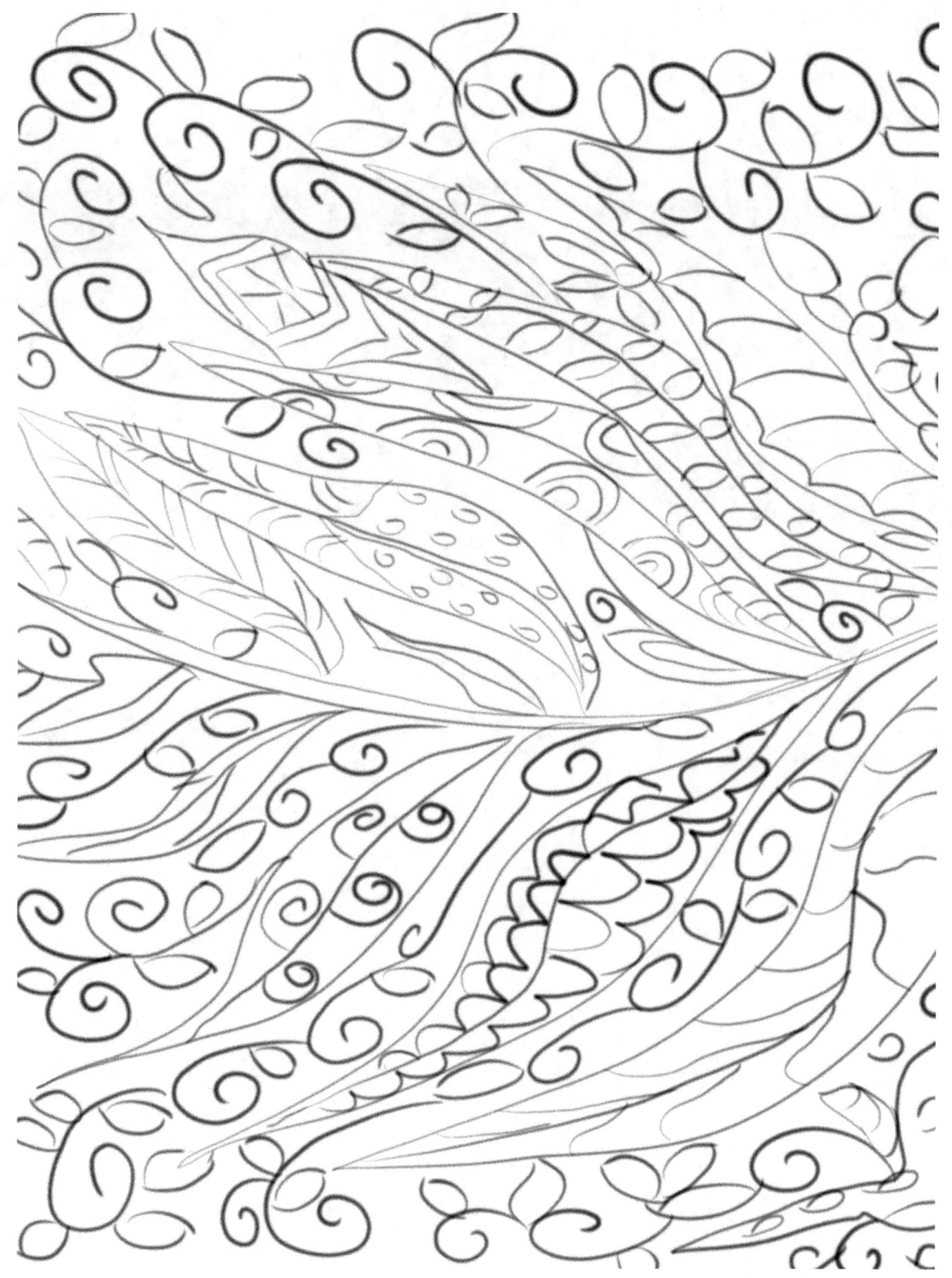

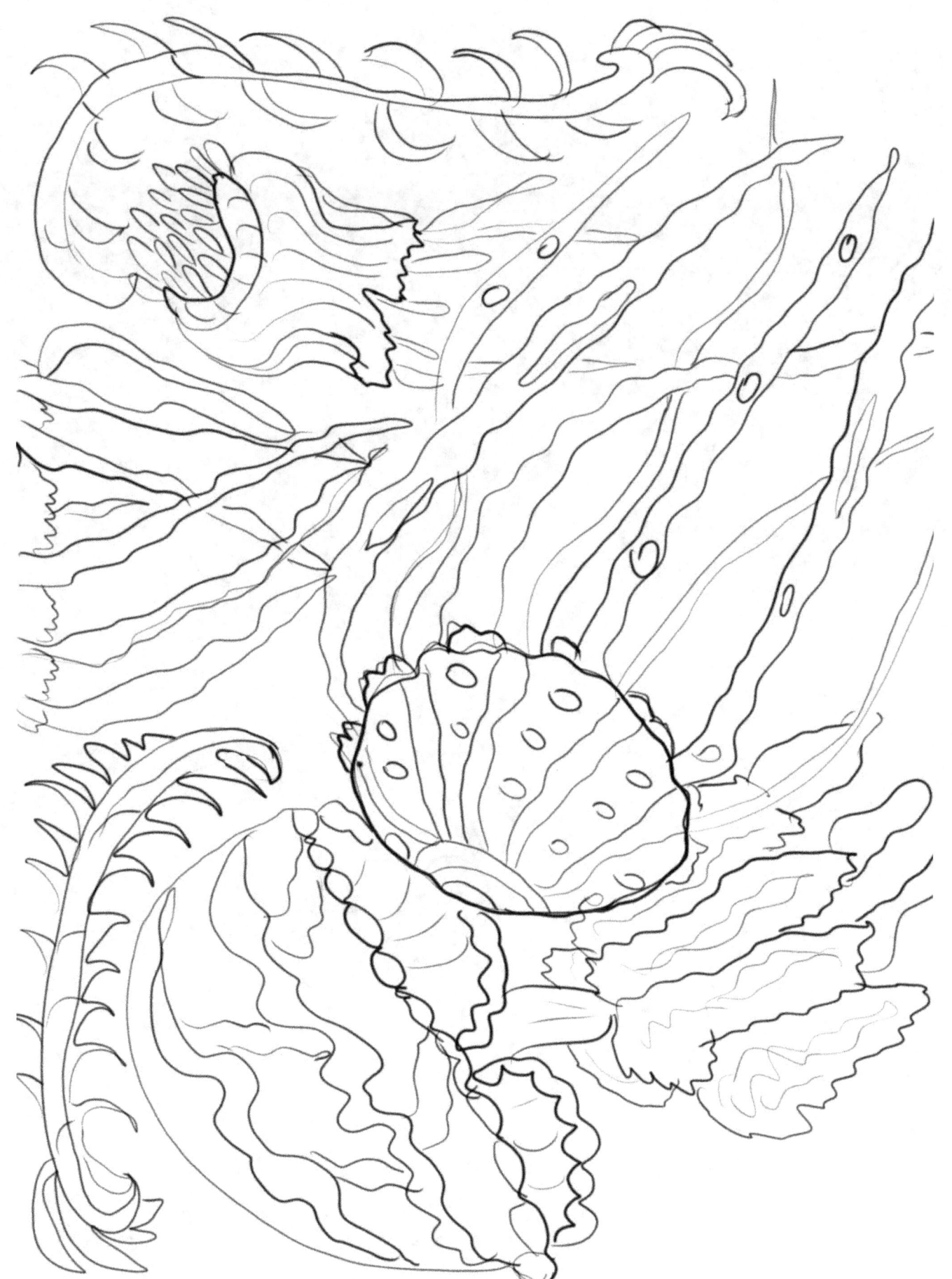

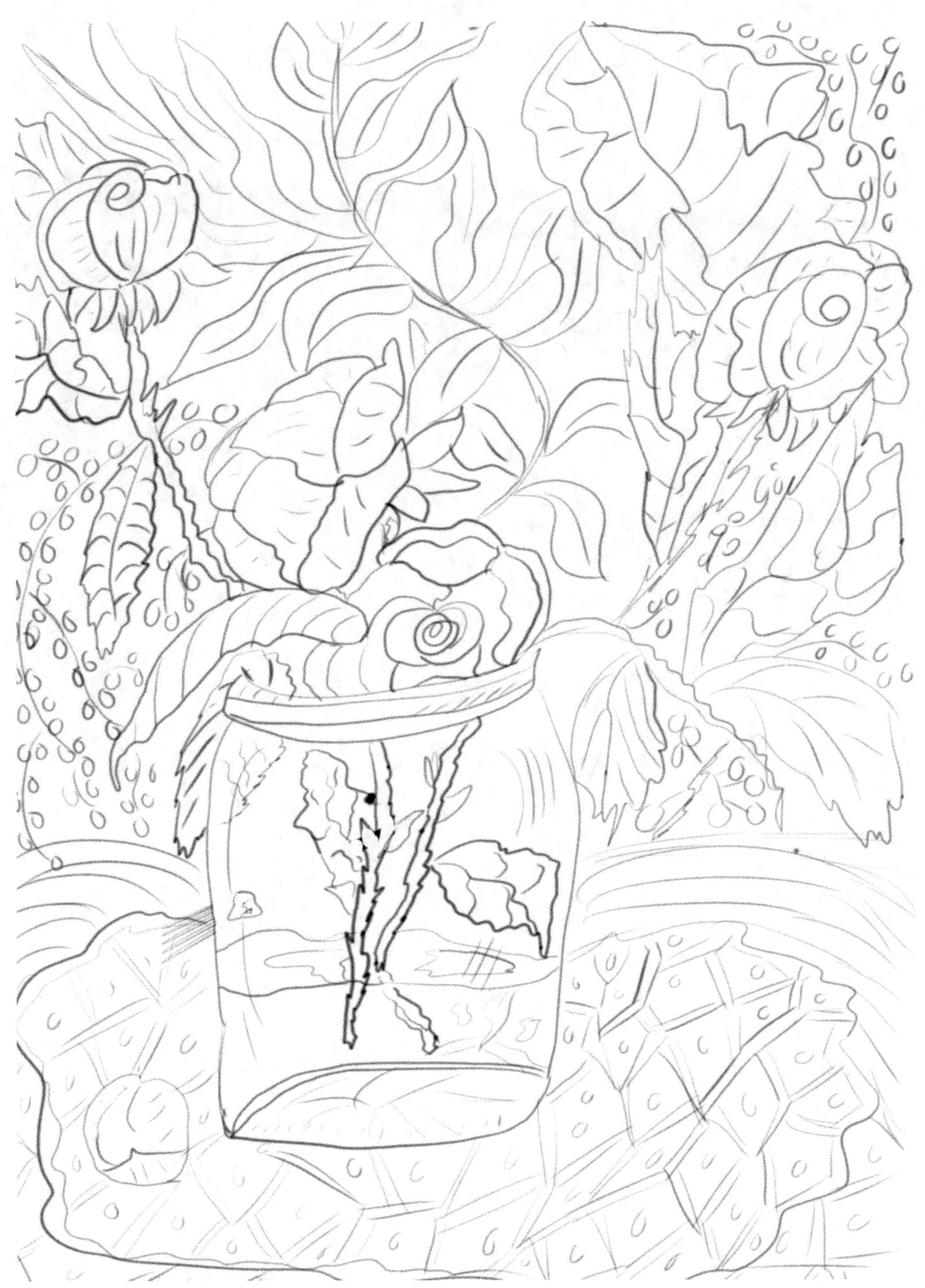

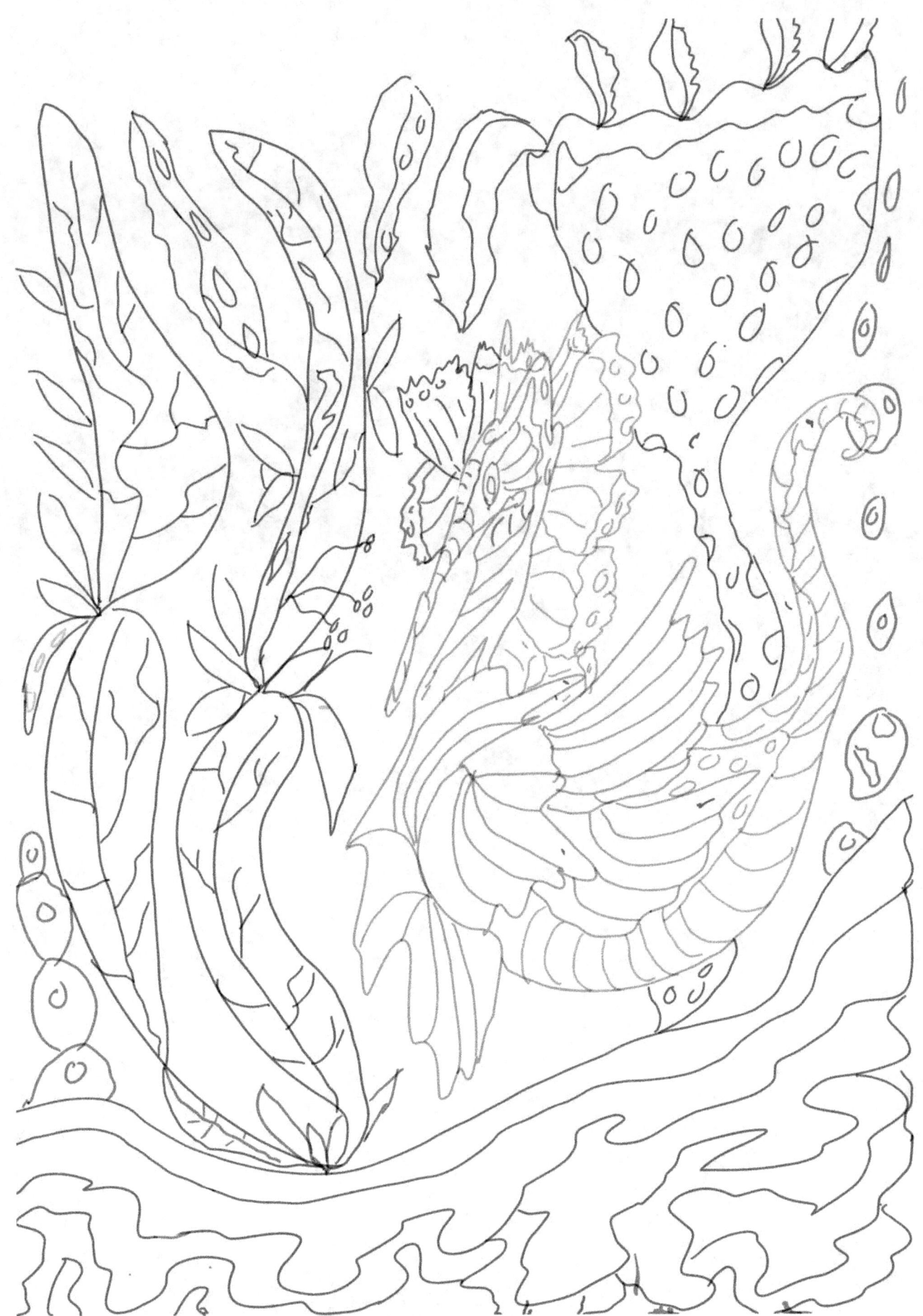

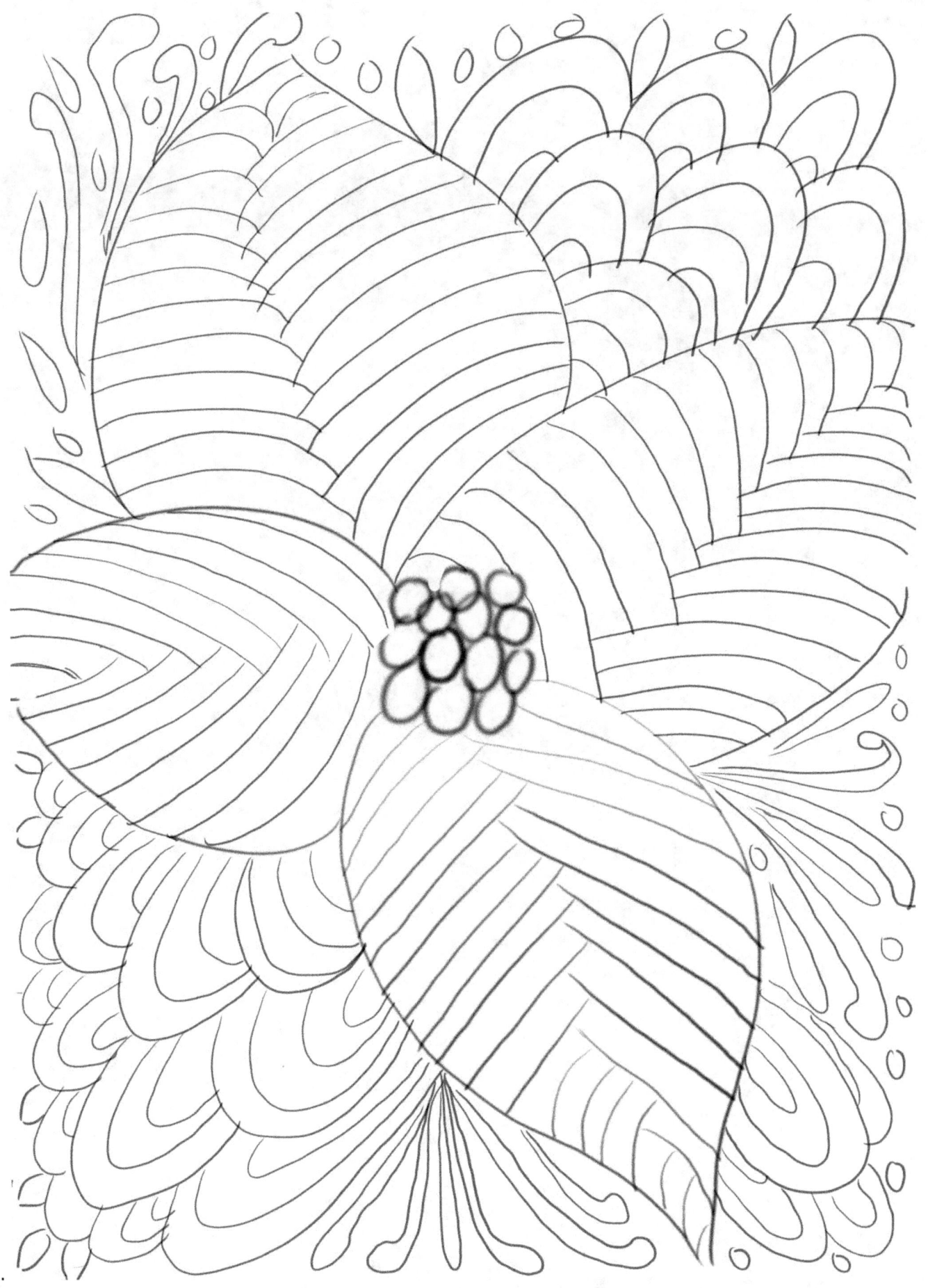

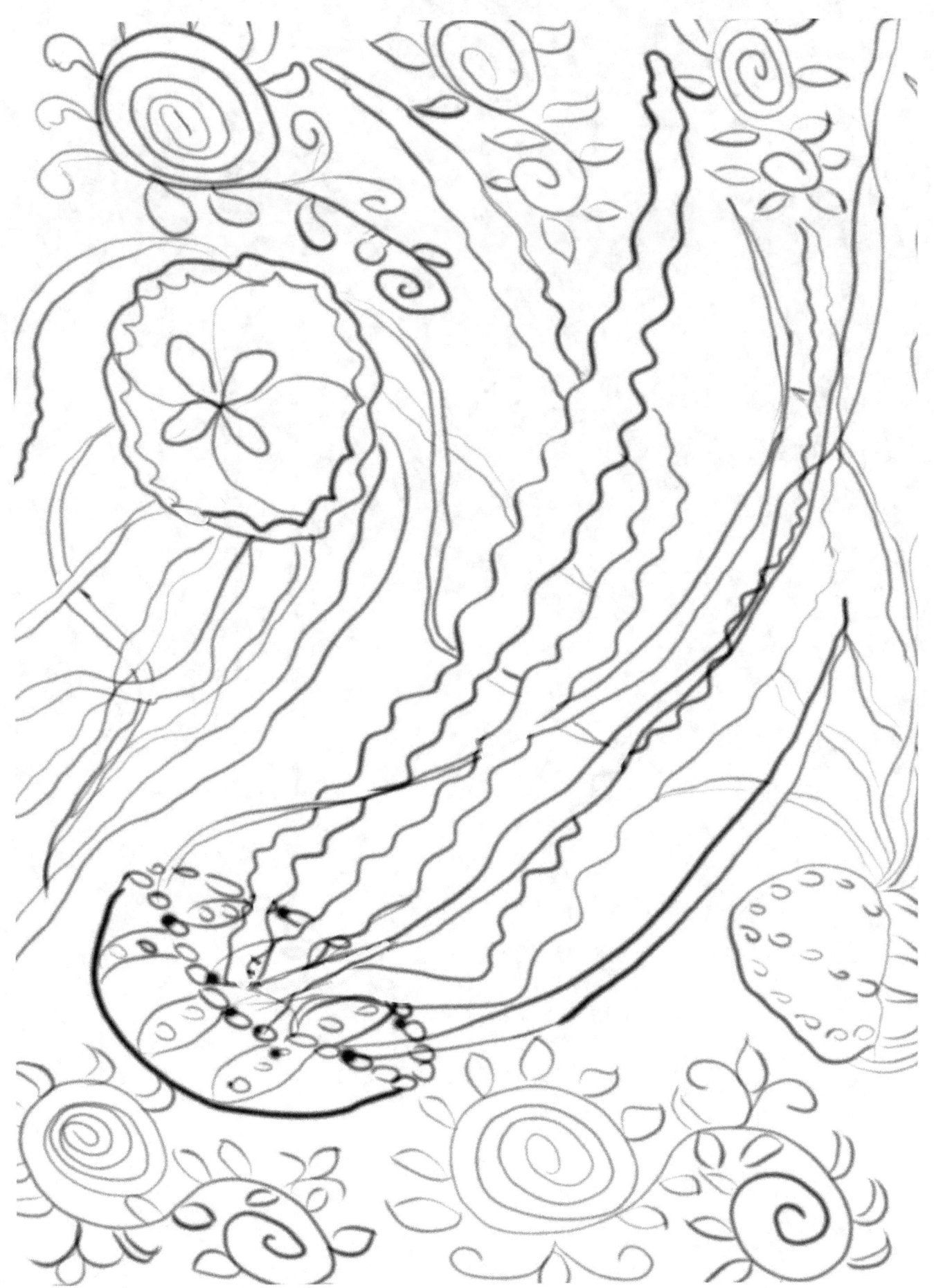

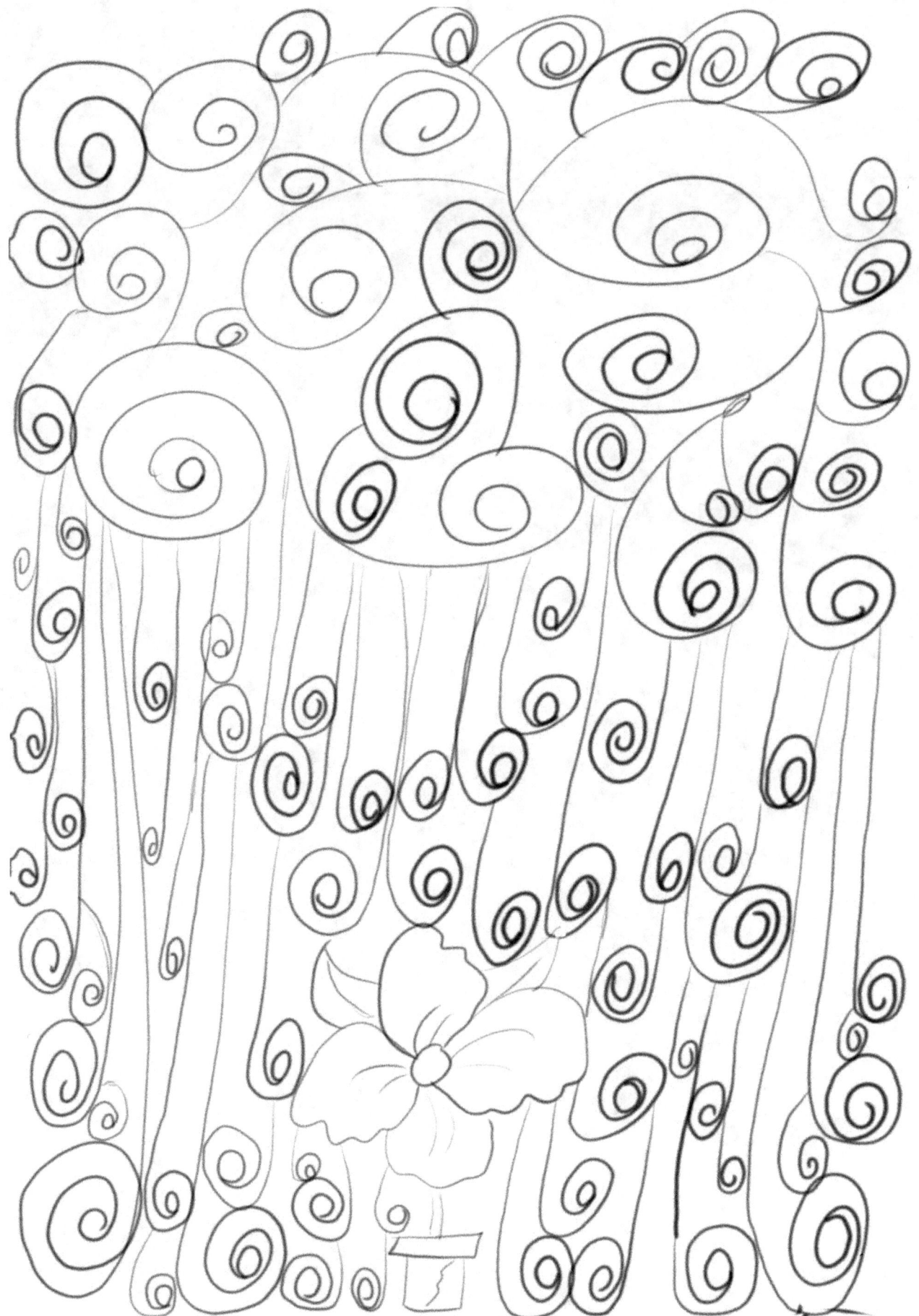

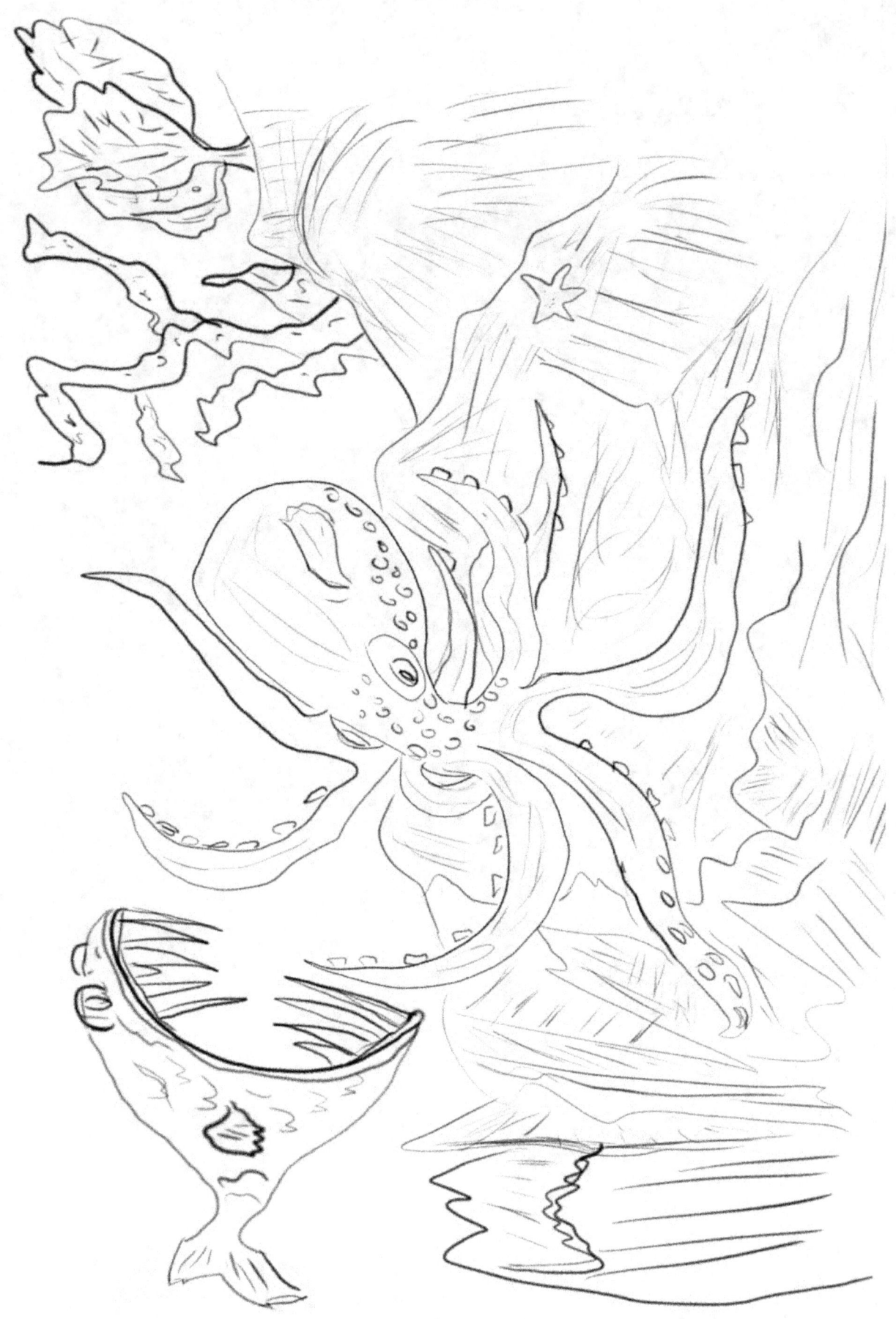

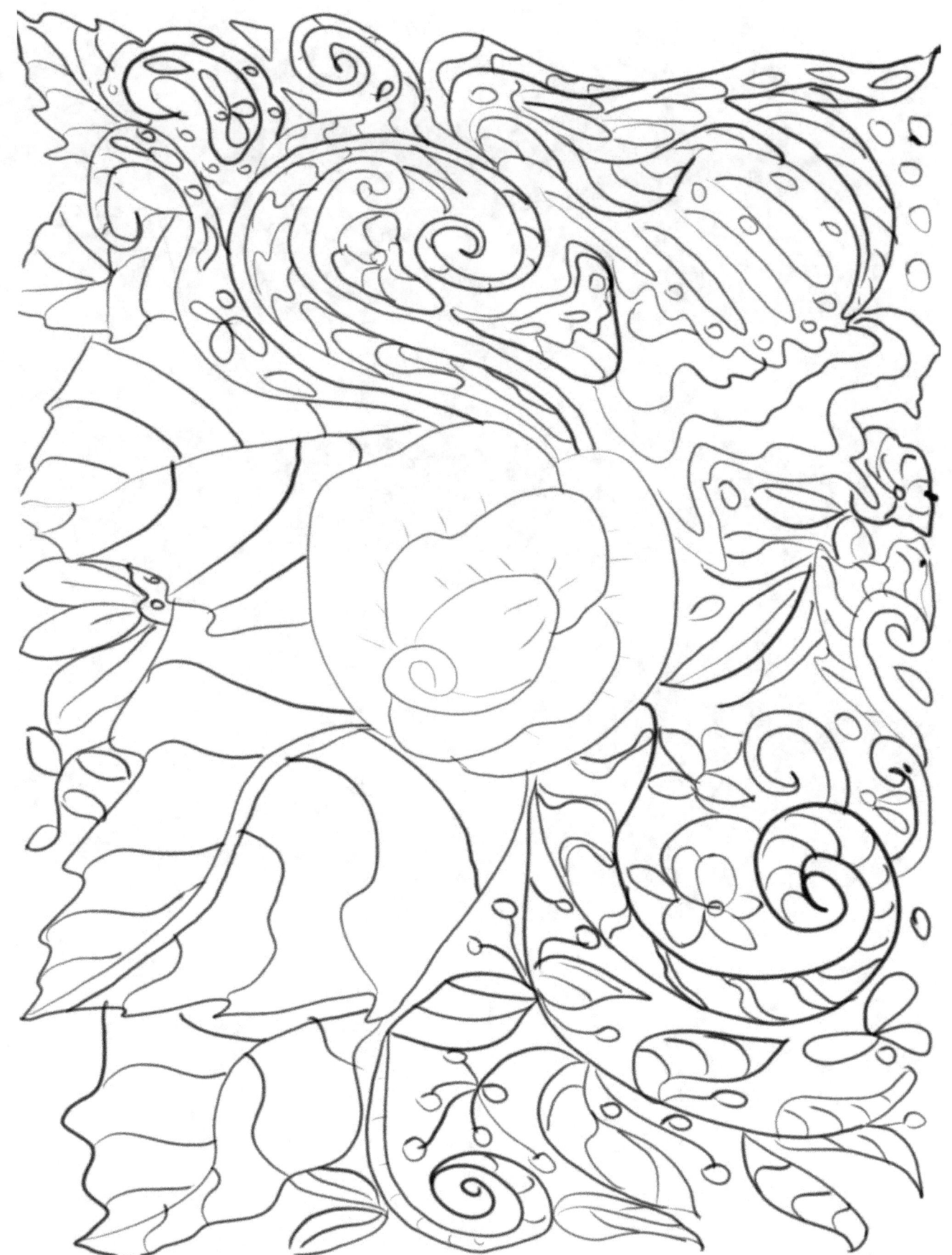

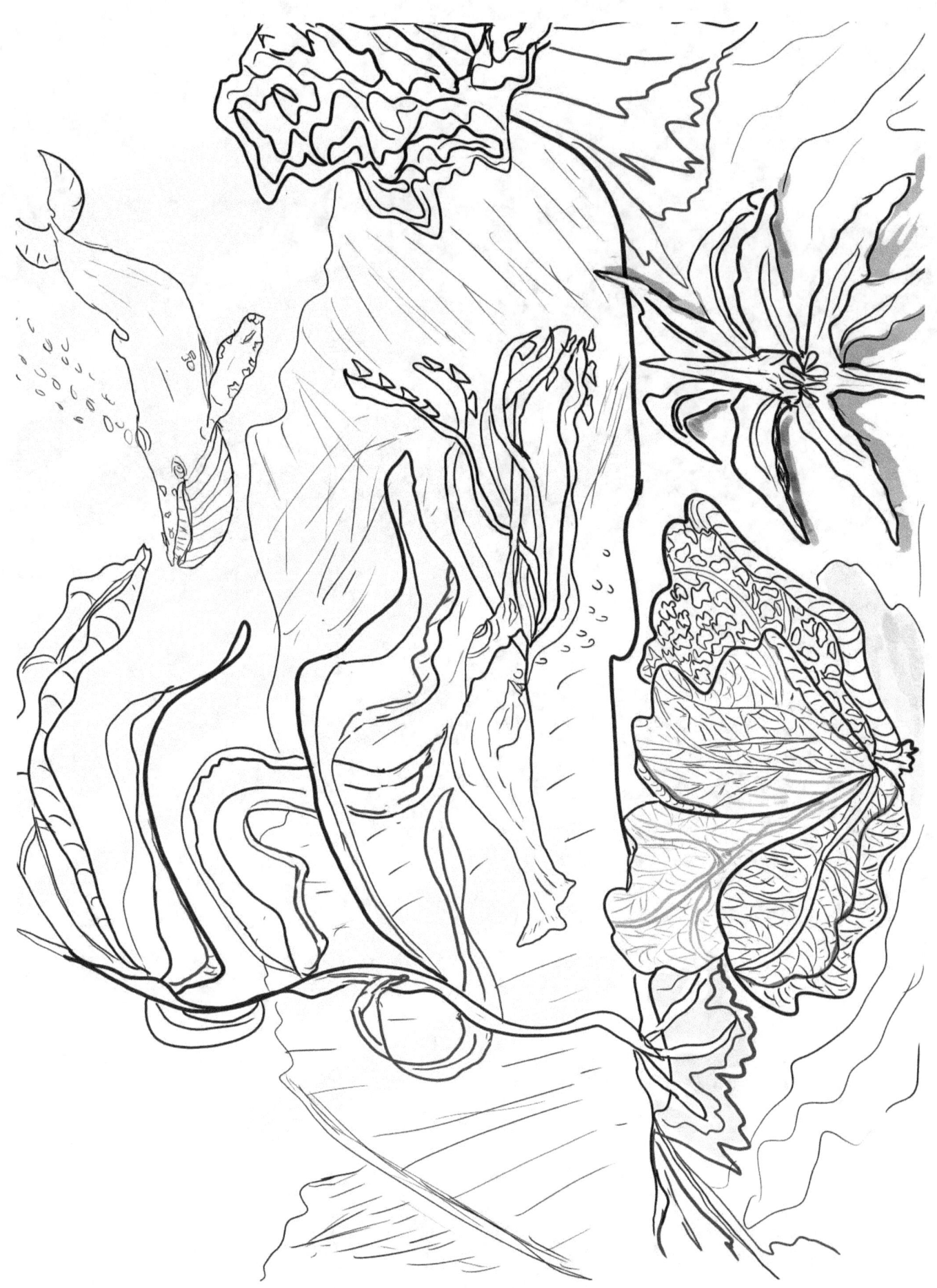

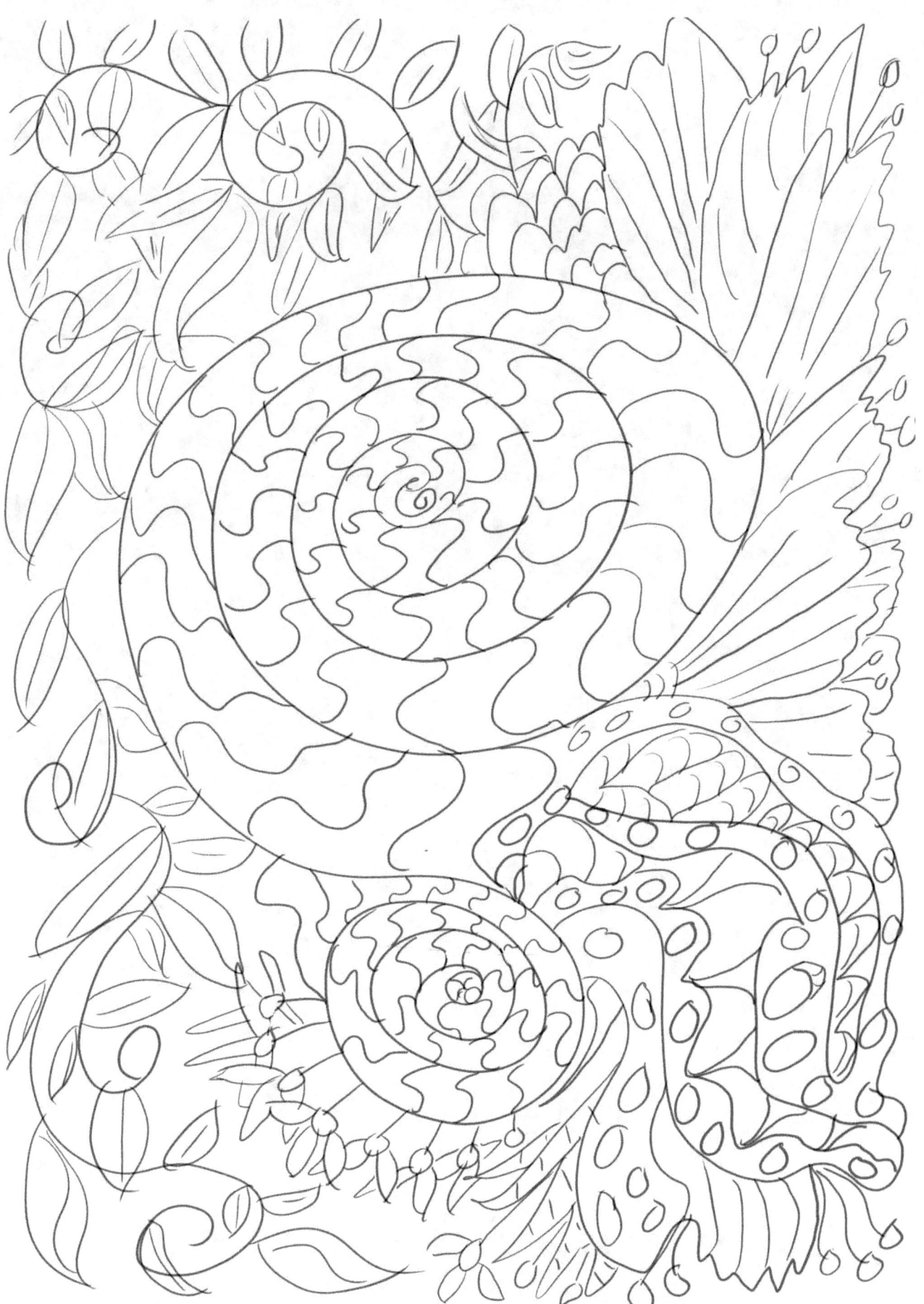

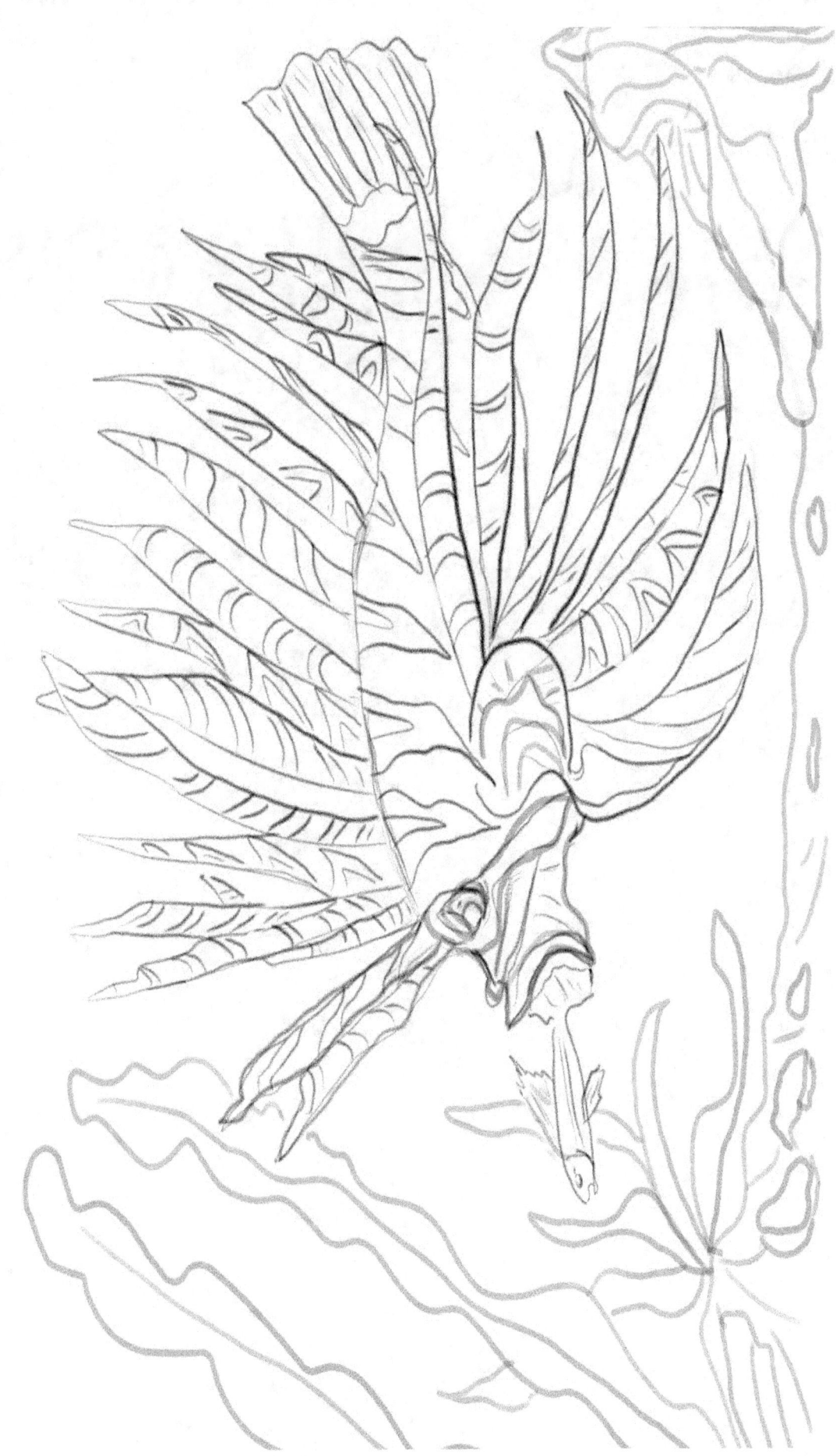

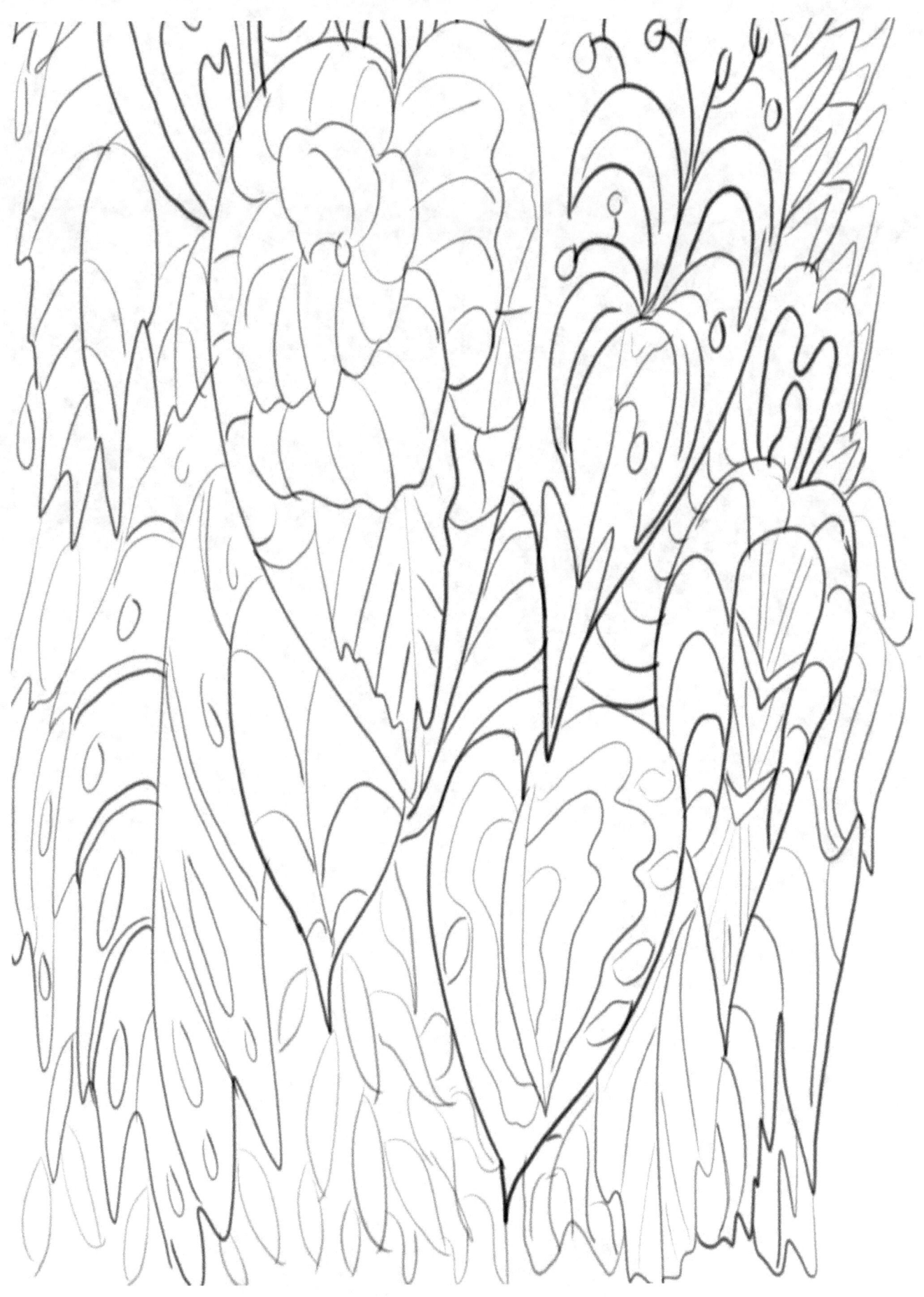

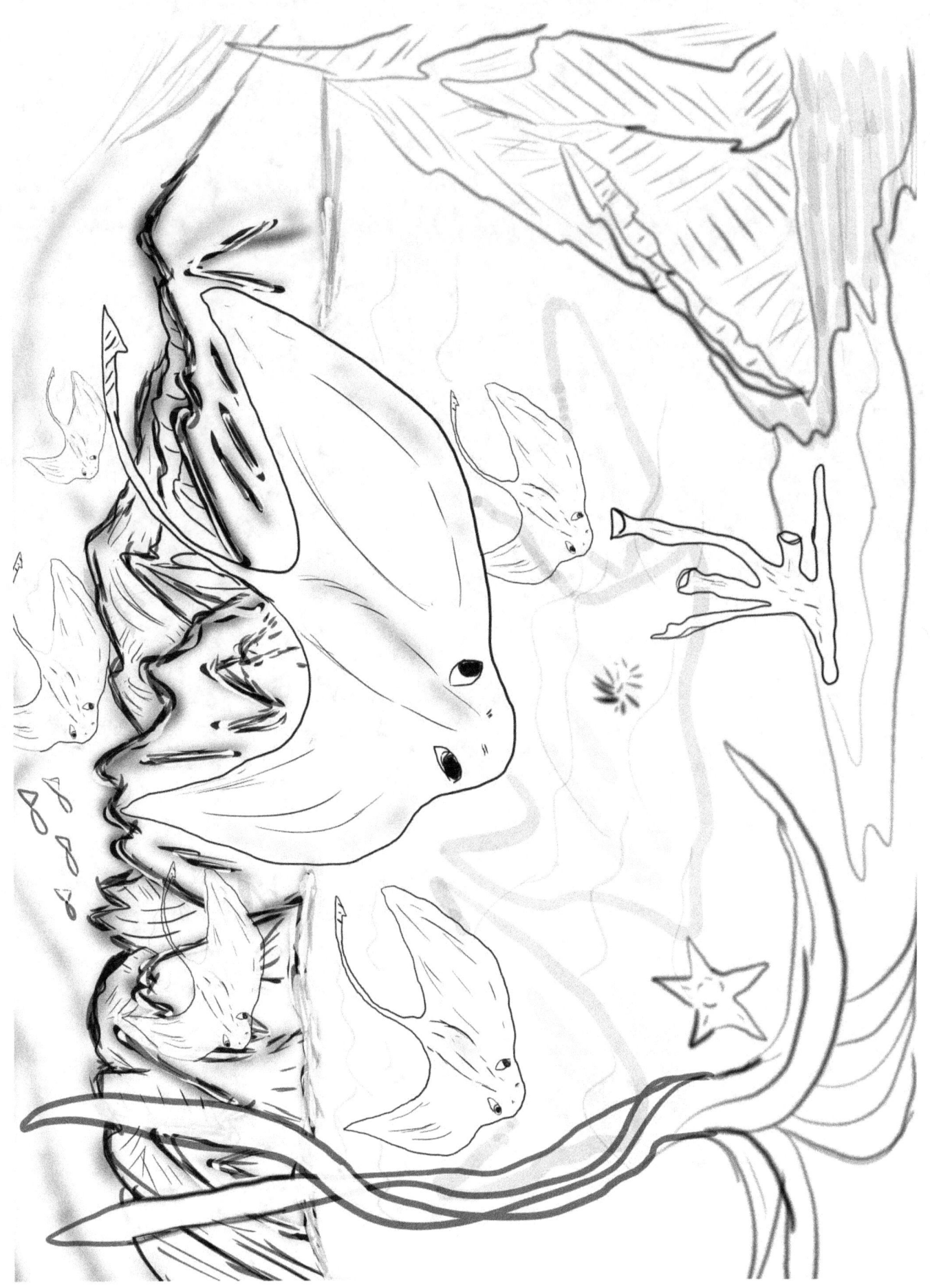

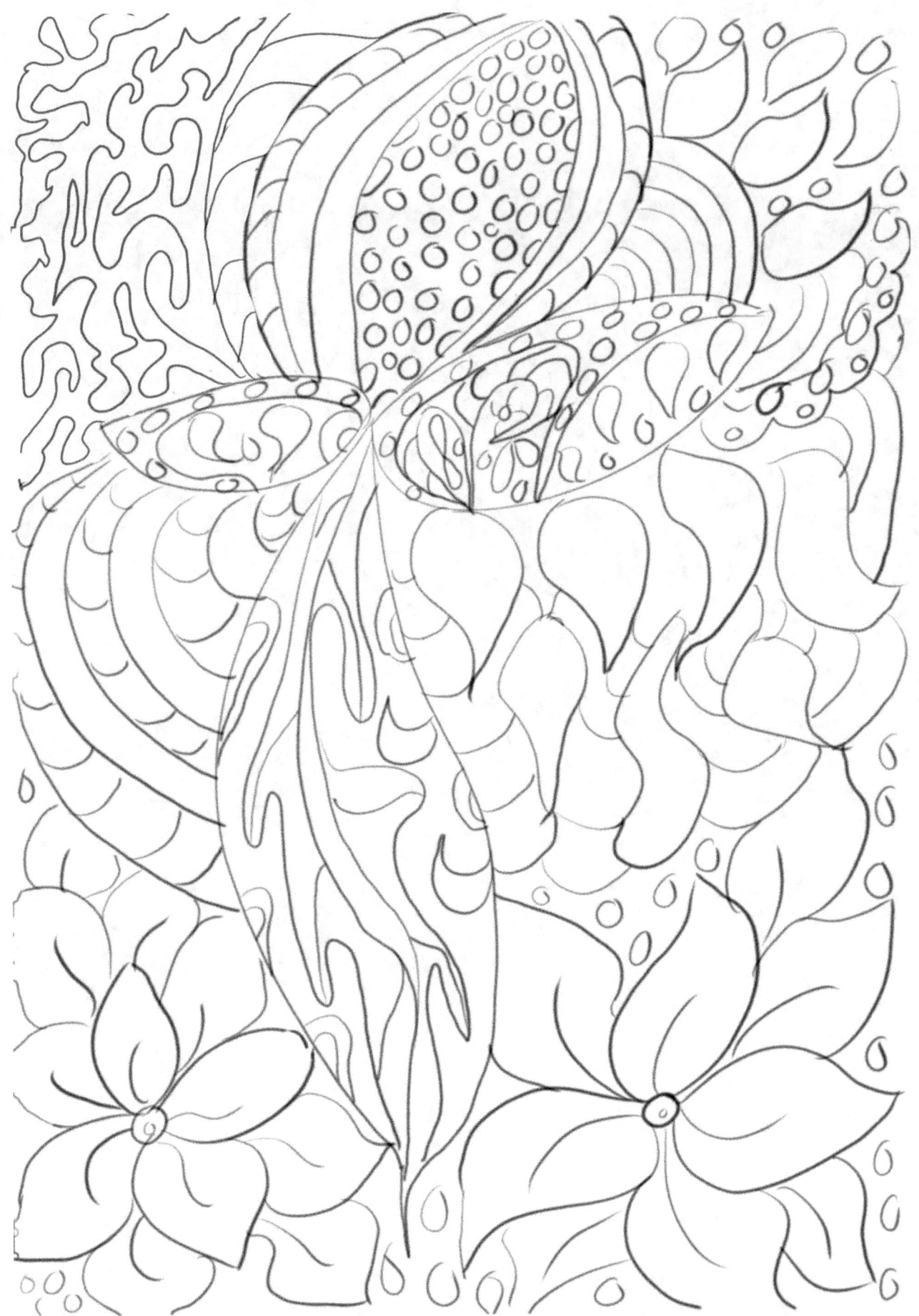

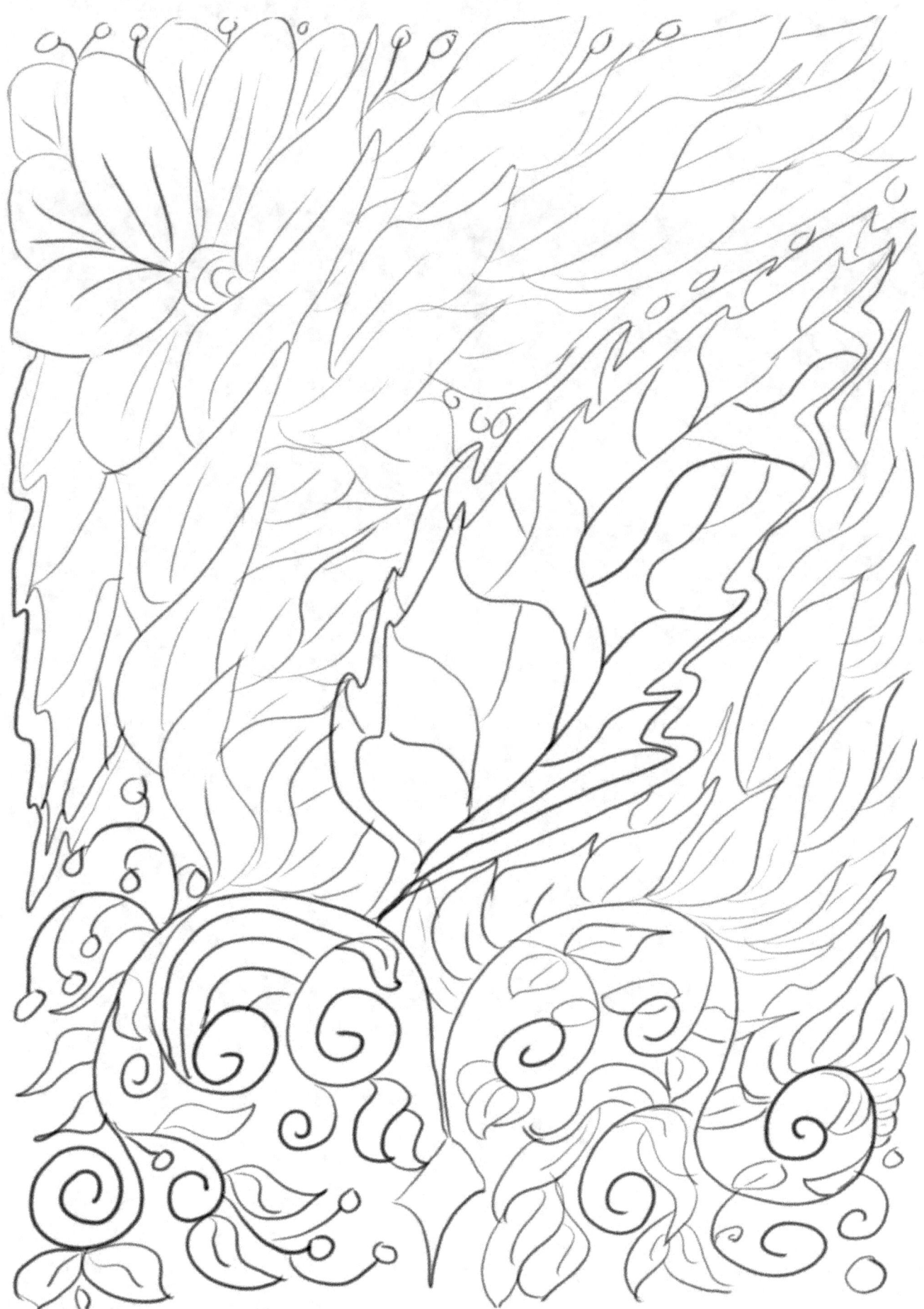

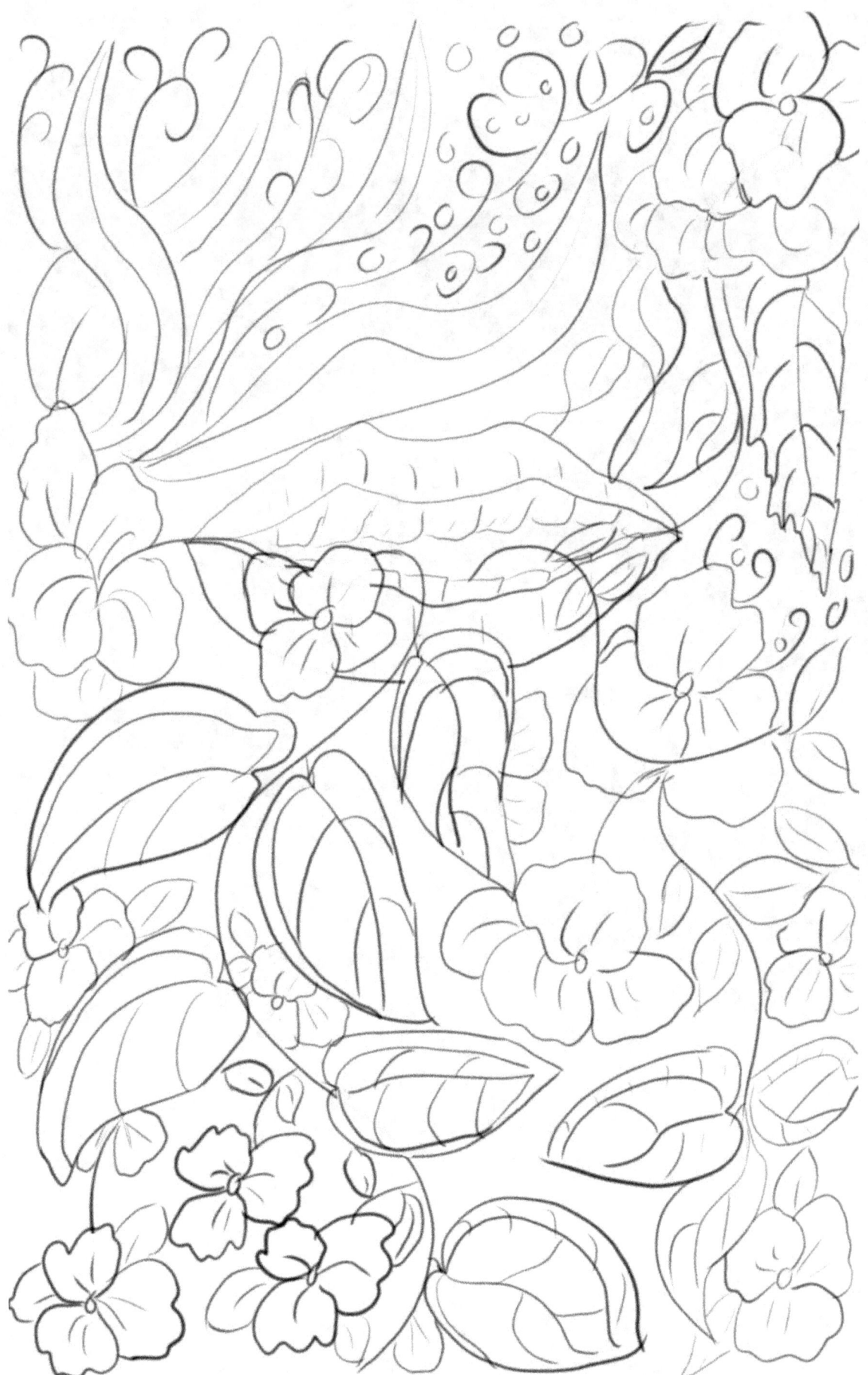